MW00685454

SKATEBOARD

SKATEBOARD

A STEP-BY-STEP GUIDE TO IMPROVING YOUR TECHNIQUE

S T E V E N **K** A N E

A QUINTET BOOK

produced for
GALLERY BOOKS
An imprint of W.H. Smith Publishers Inc.
112 Madison Avenue
New York, New York 10016

ISBN 0-8317-7853-9

This book was designed and produced by
Quintet Publishing Limited
6 Blundell Street
London N7 9BH

Creative Director: Peter Bridgewater
Designer: Ian Hunt
Editor: Shaun Barrington
Photographer: Frankie Shea

Typeset in Great Britain by
Central Southern Typesetters,
Eastbourne
Manufactured in Hong Kong by
Regent Publishing Services Limited
Printed in Hong Kong by
South Sea Int'l Press Ltd.

CONTENTS

Introduction

CESS SLIDE:
TIM JACKSON
Jackson is a pro with Dogtown Skates, Santa Monica, famous for his street skating.

We are in the residential area of a large city somewhere in the world. The weather is fine and dry, school is out for the summer.

Down the street comes a boy on a board with wheels. The wheels sing out a rhythm on the paving like a small train. There is a loud "clack!" and he's in the air. Although there is no visible means of attachment the board rises too, as if held there by a force unknown to science.

"Clack" again and they land. "Screech" and the board is now progressing down the smooth paving sideways with the skater facing downhill and slowing from "way too fast" to "fast enough". The rhythm picks up speed as a foot comes down to scoot. It comes down again on a low post before the garden fence. A gloved hand controls the board as it's propelled over the fence into the front yard – down the path and in through the screen door at the side of the house.

A battered station wagon draws up and two more arrive, their clothes festooned with the same slogans as the decals covering the crazed paintwork of the car.

The windscreen is cracked, someone has been riding on the car, but soon they are all in it with a cool bag full of tins and a beat box replacing the rhythm noise of the skate wheels. The wagon heads for the freeway and the edge of town.

Less than an hour later the car has bumped in through the gate of a farmer's field and tucked itself out of sight against a belt of trees. The crew are through the hedge. In the middle of the thicket, that once was the garden of a wealthy house, is a swimming pool. There is only a small dirty puddle in the bottom. One bails out the puddle with an old plastic sack while the others throw out cans or sweep.

Soon they stand and admire their work. Then a board is underfoot and with a flash of coloured shirt against fading blue tiles one is up on the wall of the pool tearing around like a wall of death rider. With a roar the metal axle of the board makes savage contact with the pool coping. Whoops of joy rise up from the crew. These are skateboarders; tomorrow they will be on some ramp against a wall, or maybe punishing the kerbs on some street, or shooting a hill in the cool evening.

Where did it all begin? How do they do it? Can I try? Here are the answers to these and other questions.

Tony Alva and Jef Hartsel (bottom) at the Ghost Bowl; Hartsel is a pro with S.M.A. from "Dogtown", Santa Monica, Alva is one of the original Z-boys – and a bad boy he was too – but now he's all grown up with his own skateboard company.

Tools of the Trade

An engineer has described the skateboard as the simplest way yet devised of putting a human on two wheels. He was probably right but let's not mistake simplicity for lack of refinement: a skate is a subtle blend of structure and materials that demands a high level of design and manufacture. Many of the best people in the business have come out of the aerospace industry.

THE DECK

The largest part of the thing is the board itself, often referred to as the deck. Almost without exception, serious skateboard decks are made from seven plies of Canadian or American maple glued together under heat and pressure in a large press. The most obvious feature is the upturned tail, known as the kick-tail. The nose at the front overhangs, and is itself slightly upswept.

STREET BOARDS:

NATAS, VALLEY, JESSE, DOUGLAS, GONZ, ROSCOP

The sides of the deck are curved upward to make the surface concave, a property known as "cave". This shape was something of a breakthrough when it was discovered in the early eighties, and has vastly improved the manageability of a modern skate.

The top surface is mostly covered in abrasive tape or "Griptape". This is to improve your grip on the deck, as the friction between the soles of your shoes and the surface of the deck is the essence of controlling a skateboard. The whole thing is generally stained or painted and varnished, with a bold "graphic" on the underside.

TRUCKS

The truck is the really clever part of the skateboard. A truck is not just a means of joining a set of wheels to a deck, it has a subtler function: to transfer a rocking motion of the deck into a steering motion of the wheels. The truck achieves this by pivoting at an angle to the surface of the deck. The motion is moderated and a self-centering effect is caused by the cushions. These are no longer made of rubber but of the more durable urethane. With correctly adjusted cushions the truck should spring back to the centre once pressure to turn is released. Mess around with your trucks, see how they work.

The bit of truck that is bolted to the deck is called a baseplate. The piece that moves is the hanger. The large bolt with the cushions threaded onto it that holds the whole thing together is known as the truck bolt or kingpin. The axle is called an axle, and the bit of the hanger that pivots in the baseplate is called the pivot. Simple isn't it? Between the pivot and hole it pivots in, is a plastic cup called a pivot cup.

Conveniently, the holes that take the fixing bolts are a standard pattern that is common to all pro skateboards throughout the world, as is the diameter of the kingpin and of the axle. This means that any manufacturer's wheels and trucks will fit any deck.

WHEELS

The wheels are made of polyurethane which is a very strong and "springy" plastic. They come in a variety of harnesses and sizes. Generally the very hardest are for the smoothest surfaces while the softer ones go faster and ride smoother on the rough.

VERT BOARDS:
BOYLE, DOUGLAS, WEBSTER, MILLER, CABALLERO

FREESTYLE BOARDS:
BROWN, MYER, ANDRE, RODNEY, MULLEN

All skateboard wheels use a standard pair of bearings, known as a 608. They were originally meant for use in washing machines and vacuum cleaners and the like. They were the first size of "precision bearings" to be tried in skateboard wheels back in the seventies, and they have been proved to be just the job, if they are looked after. Most people use a little spacer to keep the bearings the correct distance apart and to spread the sideways load between them.

A lot of people have a couple of tough strips of plastic on the underside of the deck. These are "rails" and serve as something to grab onto and also make the board slide easily across a variety of surfaces without destroying the bottom of the deck. It is cheaper to replace a couple of plastic strips than the whole deck. The rails are generally screwed on, although manufacturers of decks expect you to use special bolts to help prevent weakening of the wood. This makes it easier to replace the rails as well.

In many ways the history of skateboarding development is a history of materials science. A skate is by no means just any old bit of plywood with any old plastic wheels connected to it by some kind of metal axle.

WHY MAPLE?

Well, the maple tree is a great American tree, that grows best in the lands first settled by the Fathers of America, and its foliage is a major

part of the famous colors of a New England Fall: which is nothing to do with why its wood should be chosen for a great American sporting machine.

A skateboard has to be both strong, in that it must support your weight, and tough. Toughness is about being subjected to sudden and frequent shock loadings, as when you land on it from a great height, without deterioration. Not only this but it must be light and resist persistent heavy grinding on stone, brick, metal and concrete on all its edges and surfaces. Myriad fancy high tech space age materials have been tried. But only maple ply, sometimes with a little fiber-glass or carbon fiber between a couple of the plies, has stood the test.

Boards are pressed in batches of five or six in heavy industrial presses. They emerge as crude rectangles or "blanks". These are cut to the shape specified usually by a top "pro" rider, and have their truck mounting holes drilled on a jig to keep everything in line and true. At this stage they are varnished. Any colouring usually comes from a stain in the outer plies of the pressing. This is better than paint as it does not wear off and is lighter. They are then varnished to keep the water out and give a shiny finish for you to grind off on the curb.

In another part of the plant, or perhaps in another factory, they are screen-printed with the pro's own unique graphics. This may involve printing with as many as a dozen different colours on a dozen different screens. The finished decks are packed together in boxes and shipped all over the world.

TRUCK INDEPENDENTS:
GULLWING, THUNDERS, VENTURE, INDYS, G & S

WHEELS:
POWELL & SANTA CRUZ

METAL

Most truck hangers are made of a light and strong aviation grade alloy of aluminum or occasionally magnesium. These strong alloys are thick and viscous even when melted, and are thus harder to pour into molds than the runnier but weaker alloys used in cheap things like pans etc. Casting a truck in a foundry is a hot and hard job demanding experience and skill to get a consistent product. Axles should be of a "high spring" steel that will not bend easily, while the kingpins need to be resistant to the weakness that comes over metals when they are constantly loaded and unloaded. Special grades of steel resistant to metal fatigue are used in the best truck bolts.

Cushions of varying hardnesses are available. The nuts that hold it all together are nylocs, which means they have a special nylon insert to prevent them loosening. Sometimes the baseplates are made of plastic for lightness. This is either nylon or a similar plastic. These can suffer from weakness in cold weather (less than 40°F). The best are made of fiber-glass-reinforced nylon. This appears to be as near indestructible under normal conditions as it is possible to be. Experiments have been made with truck hangers in exotic plastics. These can be vulnerable to grinding on curbs and metal coping, but are very light and strong in other ways.

Some trucks are made of steel; these grind wonderfully, but because

SHOES:
(LEFT TO RIGHT) VANS HI-TOP, AIRWALK, AIRWALK PROTOTYPE, MADRID VAN, VISION STREETWEAR

they have to be welded up from a number of pieces they are vulnerable to minute defects in the welding invisible to the eye. The lightness and grindability of steel hangers has, however, won them a firm following. Trucks are one of the areas of skate design still open to development. Special replacement kingpins are available that are stronger and have a better shaped top. They are made of a steel alloy with even greater fatigue resistance and are not cheap.

URETHANE

The replacement of steel or clay wheels with loose roller bearings with polyurethane wheels on precision bearings, in the mid-seventies, was the single most important development in skate history. Urethane runs smooth and quick over a variety of surfaces, and can be made to last well.

The hardness of a wheel is measured by the engineers with a device called a durometer, and is given in a scale from 1–100. Most wheels fall in the range 80–99 with the majority around 92–97. The figure always has an 'A' after it to show the particular scale of hardness used.

Very hard wheels are favored for their speed on very smooth surfaces like metal or wood ramps, and for their even slides. Unfortunately, extreme hardness is not easy to achieve without some loss of bounce, and this resilience is important if you want speed on a rougher surface. Most skaters settle for something between 92A and 95A on the street with something harder for the ramp. Very soft wheels are used for road racing and just riding on rough terrain. These are generally around 78–85A.

Bearings vary in price and quality, but as they are very difficult to keep in tip-top condition, a moderate quality precision 608 bearing with metal shields is fine for fine weather and clean riding zones. Some folk shell out more neoprene-sealed bearings that keep the wet and dust out and the lubricating oil or grease in. Fanatics experiment with fancy greases and lubricants. Perhaps the best discovery has been completely synthetic greases and oils that are not mineral based and do not spray or wash off easily, thus protecting and cooling the bearing surfaces in all conditions. These are still hard to come by and most people are content to make do with a standard oil or grease. Heavy grease stays on well but the wheels do not run so easily at low loads and speeds. Lighter oils are harder to keep on. Take your choice.

The best rails are made of a fancy plastic called Ultra High Molecular Weight Polyurethane, or UHMWP to its friends. This stuff is made of very long chain molecules that resist being worn away, and slide over rough surfaces well. The same plastic is stuck in the bottom of vast truck hoppers to stop stones wearing them away, and is several times more durable than steel in this type of situation.

PLASTICS:
CELLBLOCK, POWELL RAILS & TAILSAVER

Skate History

The first skateboard could have been anywhere. Right since the beginning of the century kids must have got an old pair of roller skates and screwed them onto a bit of wood, and first sat and then stood on it.

It was in the late fifties that someone made the analogy with surfing and people started making purpose-built skateboards with hardware borrowed from rollerskates. At this time there was the first small "craze", mainly confined to California and a few other areas. It was very much seen as something for surfers to do when there was no surf.

SMITHGRIND:
BOB BOYLE (REGULAR)
Grinds and slides were impossible with the early claywheel boards. Neither the wheels nor the boards could stand treatment like this.

People just got off on rolling around, probably imitating the easier surfing moves and just going as fast as possible (which was not very) until the old clay rink wheels or even steel wheels gave out and they had to buy another set secondhand from a rollerskate rink. At about the same time kids in Rio de Janeiro in Brazil were nailing old truck wheel bearings onto planks and racing them down the steep roads of Sugarloaf Mountain.

Most people lost interest in this first wave of skating because it was limited in appeal. The boards were too slow and couldn't be maneuvered with any style. It wasn't until the mid-seventies until someone noticed that the new urethane wheels that had been a flop for roller skates in a rink were the business on a skateboard. The next wave came all in a rush. The pioneers were undoubtedly the Californians in general and the kids in Venice and Santa Monica, and particularly their older mentors left over from the first wave.

Early claywheel board: life expectancy – severely limited.

Kicktails were invented, big races like the Catalina Classic were staged. The Hester series of vert riding comps sprung into being and suddenly, Hey Presto: we had an industry on our hands. The Companies involved were a fusion of surf board companies and some roller skate and cycle firms. The staff of *Surfer* magazine restarted *Skateboarder* and we seemed set for a worldwide explosion.

Fortunes were won and lost. But more importantly, people discovered vertical riding in pools and on ramps and got air out of them. Just as the "craze" was fizzling out the next big innovative leaps were made. Wide decks, concave decks and the ollie were the big leaps. Flat-bottomed ramps helped to ease the arrival of all the new moves that sprang from them.

How did these things speed the onward rush of skating? First, wide concave boards were just so much more controllable, as there was some margin for error in landing things for a start. Ollie flips, as they were first called, enabled people to get up onto and out of things without having to use one of the dodgy ways of attaching your feet to the deck, or grabbing with their hands. Ollies on the vert were at first just no-hands airs floated out and carefully brought back in by arranging for the feet and deck to go in more or less the same direction. After flatland ollies were being popped, people started to gain confidence in controlling the trajectory of the board.

Flat-bottomed half-pipes gave more time between sides, and incidentally eased the sharing of ramps with BMX bikes, something which cut both ways in the lean times. Hard-capped knee pads cut down on injuries.

When people started to get interested again skating was ready for them this time: there were hot videos of the new-style skating ready to spread the word and the styles too. By 1986 skating was well on the way back in the USA and was beginning to revitalize the isolated pockets of hardcore enthusiasts who had been struggling on in isolation in other continents. Foreigners came to California to join in the boom and take the good news back home.

By 1988 skating was back worldwide and spreading into countries that never saw it first or second time around. The sport now has all the air of something that has fully arrived, and the existence of adult skaters in the business gives the trade a loyalty it never had in the seventies, when people fled to BMX and rollerskating as soon as the wind blew that way.

SMITHGRIND:
MARK G & S (GOOFY)
The early Z-boys would have been astounded that knee pads, skate gloves and helmets would become essential gear a decade on.

Shut Up and Skate!

OK, so how do we start? Get the best skateboard you can get your feet on. The smoothest flat area. Watch out for those little stones that jam the wheels.

There are several different ways to get onto the skate and get it moving. Don't think about it yet: just make sure that you wind up with your feet roughly over each truck, so you are standing sideways. Which foot you put on first, and which foot you put in front, is up to you. There are hot skaters using each of the four permutations.

1 Right foot on the front – push off with the left and put it on the back.

2 Left foot on the front push off with the right and wind up facing the opposite way to the first method. These two are called respectively: Regular foot stance with back foot shunting or Goofy foot stance with

REGULAR FOOT PLACEMENT

back foot shunting. The other two methods are regular or goofy, but putting the back foot on first and pushing ("shunting") with the front.

Just get on the board in the way which feels most natural to you. It's best to start with back foot shunting as the skateboard doesn't run away from you. When you first start, aim for a fast walking pace. Get this! Don't push the board away from you and try and get on it. This is not the way! Send yourself forward, and take the board with you.

As you go along, lean the way you want to go, and steer the deck by leaning it so it comes with you. This distinction sounds pedantic but believe me it is the key. You are not driving something like a car. You are gliding along and the skateboard is there between you and the ground to cut out the friction. If you get this image of what you are doing firmly in your mind, everything is a lot easier.

Stopping: at first you can just jump off in a panic, but once you are a little practiced you can lean back a touch while dropping your shunting foot to the ground and using it as a brake. From slow speeds you just stop yourself with your foot firmly down, as if you were running, but at higher speeds skid your shoe on the surface. It helps if you drop your whole weight to some degree onto the braking foot rather than timidly dabbing it down. The result is more effective and controllable.

If you fall don't stick your arm out to break your fall, you are more likely to break your arm. Wear some

PUSHING OFF REGULAR

SHANE O'BRIEN

Leave your front foot in the normal position. Push the board with the back foot on the floor level with the back wheels. The more speed you need the more extended your leg should be. Get back on the board as soon as you run out of leg. Do not stall otherwise you'll do the splits.

PUSHING OFF WITH THE FRONT FOOT:

BOD BOYLE

This is the style for people who cannot ride properly like this guy. It is the same method but with the other leg.

padding and roll out. Gloves are good, as whether you like it or not you will fall on your hand at some time, even if you are just guiding yourself into a roll. If you come off going very fast indeed, try and slide on your padding to slow down enough to roll safely. Rolling at high speed is dangerous. After a while you can cotton on to sliding along on your hands, feet and butt or the other way up on knee pads and gloves.

Practice with loose trucks just steering around things, getting the feel of the skate and losing your fear of falling off. If you can find a path through a grassy park this is good because you can always bail out on-to the grass if you blow it.

As you progress you can try

1

2

3

4

5

TIC-TAC

FUN BUNCH

This can be done when moving or stationary, and saves pushing. From where your board is rolling, kickturn 45° left/right of the board's original position. Then kickturn back 90° and back again 90°, so that you are alternately heading 45° either side of your starting position. This can be done as many times as you want and as fast as you want.

"pumping," which is a method of propelling yourself along by carving a wave-like path from side to side. The way you get propulsion is to push sideways against the grip of the wheels as the board is steering across your direction of travel. Because the wheels do not want to slide sideways the force is translated into a forward motion. As you do this from side to side, visualize a fish swimming through the water. The dynamics are similar. With the fish the sideways pressure against the water is translated into forward thrust. You can adjust the angle and frequency of your 'pumping' as your speed varies. Try it first when you are already going along at least at walking pace. This makes it easier to get the hang of it.

SETTING UP A BOARD

Check your board before you start. Stand it on a thick carpet so it doesn't roll too easily and practice steering it. If the wheels can touch the deck tighten up the big truck nut. Check the wheels are tight enough not to wobble about but not so tight that they jam solid. Check that they run freely. Check yourself next. Wear thick pants so you don't get hurt. Thick leather gloves, gardening or truck loading gloves are fine at this stage if you don't have special skate gloves. Loosen up a bit before you start.

If you've got a secondhand or borrowed setup, check it even more: give everything a good tug to check all the nuts are tight. You should even check the trucks are on the right way (the cushions should be towards the middle).

USING THE TAIL

Put the board back on the carpet. Put your foot on the tail to get a feel of lifting it and turning the front from side to side. Go out and try it rolling along. Spend a day steering around by 'kickturning' like this as well as turning with the trucks.

As you progress you can use this to turn 180° from going up a slope to going down. From this it's a small step to turning on a low bank and then on a steeper ramp. Success at this stage depends upon you letting yourself come around naturally.

The tail can be used as a brake. Put the weight of your back foot onto the tail and slide it. A variation of this is to hang the back foot off the edge of the tail and slide on that.

There is a kick tail based version of "pumping" called Tic-tacking. This is similar to pumping but you are just pushing against the back wheels as you kickturn from side to side (see pics on previous page). If you do this without touching the front wheels down after each turn but instead keep them in the air, it's called Spacewalking.

You can ride off a curb just by skating off the edge by unweighting a touch and hoping you land on the same spot as the board. This is much easier and more together if you use the tail to lift the front of the deck as you go off the edge.

ACID DROP

SHANE O'BRIEN

This move is straightforward and can be done at any speed. Roll up to the edge with feet in the normal position. When rolling off, wheelie the board as the front wheels get to the edge. Land compressed to absorb the shock, don't lean back or over the board on this move.

ACID DROP

S'BANK LOCAL

When starting off, don't try too great a drop; start by riding off curbs to get your confidence and get a feel for lifting the nose of the deck by using the tail.

BANKS AND SIMPLE RAMPS

There is no doubt that a bank or ramp looks and feels daunting when you first consider riding it. But it's no big deal. Thinking about it is a whole lot tougher than doing it. Remember the principle that *you* are going up or down the bank and the board is just there between you and the surface. Steer it around by carving it up the bank and smoothly back down.

If you go up and turn so you are facing up the slope as you come around you are said to be turning "frontside." If you go the other way (ie with your butt to the top of the slope) you are turning "backside." This is the same if you are kick-turning.

Of course you don't have to turn around when you skate straight up a bank. You can just come down backwards. This is called fakieing or coming down fakie. This is weird at first as all the control is reversed. It's worth practicing as it will hold you in good stead in your first encounter with a halfpipe.

Try kickturning or carving crouched and standing up. Try rolling on the backwheels (wheely) while turning in a kind of hybrid between a kickturn and a carve. (Useful if your trucks are too tight.) Try going up to kickturn and letting the board roll back a bit before you turn, this is a rollback. Go for a full 360° instead of the simple 180° kick-turn. To do this you have to go up "fakie" and come down forwards.

As the bank or ramp gets steeper you will find it easier to crouch ("tuck") at the top, especially if the curvature is tight. This makes coming off easier and more controllable as well. Let your knees come right up to your chin if necessary in a tight spot. Later you can vary it and experiment with extending your legs to increase your height at the top. If you play around with this you can start to "vertical pump" which is another way to propel yourself: it's a bit like propelling a playground swing. Basically, you are using your legs to give you more height at the top and more speed down the slope or "transition," as it is called in skating.

FRONTSIDE CARVE

BOD BOYLE

Take this move at any speed for your own style. Hit the transition angle at about 45°, compression will help to style it. As you go up the wall, keep carve and don't take a straight line. Turn your shoulders into the rolling-out spot and put pressure on your heels for responsive independent truck movement.

BACKSIDE CARVE

SHANE O'BRIEN

This move is basically the same as the frontside carve but a little easier. Use your weight leaning over the board and your toes for board control.

FAKIE

SHANE O'BRIEN

Approach the lip with enough speed to get half the board out. You should be standing level all the way through this. As the board goes over and is ready to come in, let it in at its own pace. Look where you are going and pump on the transition maintaining normal balance.

FAKIE 360° KICK TURN

SHANE O'BRIEN

This move resembles the 360° backside slide. Go up the wall with shoulder facing the tail. When you kickturn, do it all at the same speed. Your body should be upright all the time and your shoulders ahead of the board until the last quarter – then let the board catch up. The 360° kickturn should be done stationary: no carving.

SLIDING THE WHEELS

The sliding of skateboard wheels is almost as important as their rolling. Sliding the wheels is a way of losing speed, and another method of changing direction. Slides are dramatic and sometimes noisy, and the subtle control they give over speed and direction makes other things possible and certain terrains rideable.

All this stuff is easier either with hard wheels on a smooth surface or with slightly softer ones (92A) on a rougher surface. Slides with soft wheels on a smooth surface are tough. Whatever wheels you use, you will need to switch them around the board regularly to prevent uneven wear, as sliding takes a lot out of any set of wheels.

180° FOOT SLIDE
STEVE DOUGLAS
Roll into the move with two-push speed, with your back foot over the back bolts. Take your front foot off and push the board through 180° with the back leg angled towards the nose of the board. Without letting the board go too far ahead, jump back on (by pushing off the front leg) and stand up as you would normally.

To slide you must be moving quite fast, turn the board as for a very sharp turn, but really throw it around with you yourself either going straight on, or at least turning a lot less than your wheels would like. Something has to give in this argument between the wheels trying to steer one way and you going straight on. You either fall off, or if you have got your weight low and behind the direction of travel, you slide out. Release a little of your weight from the back wheels for a rear wheel drift. In the most extreme version you just twist the whole board around 90° and keep on sliding sideways.

360° BACKSLIDE SLIDE

STEVE DOUGLAS

Speed is optional on this one. Rolling forward, spin your body through 360°. Do not take your front wheels off the floor too high. When spinning you should use your shoulders to gain momentum. Do not spin the first 180° too quickly or you won't be able to keep control.

Before you stall to a halt bring it back straight or even .take it on around 180° into a fakie. You are now going backward. Slide it around again quickly.

This kind of stuff is easier frontside, that is, turning to face the way you are traveling. Try it backside, putting your hands down on the ground (wear gloves).

Experiment with different types of slide. Some are forced hard and the wheels break out of the grip with some protest. With hard wheels on smooth terrain you can unweight a little and just slide the slippery wheels around beneath you. Try just sliding the back. Try it up and across banks. Mix slides with carves and kickturns. By balancing the downward and lateral force you can have a lot of control. Control of your weight distribution comes from relaxed but positive use of your legs as a kind of natural active suspension. Always slide with slightly bent knees, so you have some margin for control: straightening your legs for more force sideways or downwards, or bending them to unweight and slide easier, or to bring your weight back over the deck and lessen sideways force.

180° SLIDE TO FAKIE

SHANE O'BRIEN

Go into the trick at your own speed. When ready, slide your board 180° by turning your hips, shoulders and legs. Stand up all the way through the move and keep good balance. This move is best done quickly for maximum speed.

When you have practiced enough, you can head down a steep hill and drift-slide off excess speed by throwing the board around: "cess" sliding.

You cannot afford to be timid with slides. You have to be fully committed, otherwise the grip of the wheels takes over and you just pull a very tight turn into disaster. Practice heading fast into short grass and throwing the board into a long sliding drift as you hit the grass. This is very good for your confidence. Gloves are a must for slides, and hip padding is a very good idea.

FRONTSIDE OLLIE:
BOD BOYLE
Try it on the flat first.

OLLIES

The ollie is a wonderful thing. Practice is the only key to this seemingly magical trick whereby you jump up and, as if magically glued to your feet, the board comes up with you defying Newtonian physics.

There is no magic: it is just the translation of rotational momentum into vertical momentum in two simple stages.

Step one: Get your feet so one is on the tail and the other about midway between the trucks. Crouch a bit. As you jump up from the board your back foot kicks the tail down hard so it "thwacks" on the ground. The front comes up hard and fast until the deck is almost vertical.

Step two: The other foot catches the rising front of the deck with the leading edge of the foot and pushes it forwards reversing the rotation of the board and bringing the back up to join the front in the air.

The tail has already left the ground as it has itself bounced off the floor. The front foot allows the tail to swing up behind the ascending nose, catching it up.

OLLIE

SHANE O'BRIEN

Roll up to the object with any speed. Take your front foot back six inches down the board. When your front wheels come close to the object, slap the tail and jump as it hits. Simultaneously tilt your front foot so it is on its side and slide it up to your original foot placement. Always keep good central weight position, not too far in front and not too far behind. Land with all wheels together by slowly pushing your legs towards the floor as soon as you are descending on the move.

You and your board are now in the same relative position as you were at the start, only perhaps a foot or so above the ground. The feet gently shepherd the deck into line for a landing. The legs compress as you touch down. In some ways this is easier while rolling forward. The front foot bit seems to come easier to most people.

Try them on banks. Try them going backwards. Change your foot placement sideways a touch and try turning the board 180° as it rises. Practice, practice, practice if you want to get high.

OLLIE

SHANE O'BRIEN

If you never learned another move, there's practically enough satisfaction in ollieing onto, across, and over things to last a lifetime. Note that the legs are compressed in the air and then are gently straightened on the descent.

If you put one foot on the ground and use the other back foot to ollie the deck and control it, you are doing a "No Comply." I don't know why. Do them up kerbs. Turn the board 180° and its called a "forty three."

Ollies are not just for impressing other skaters: they are for getting onto things and back off them. Onto a bench or a bank with a kerb at the bottom, or off the top of a little jump ramp, over a nasty broken bit of widewalk, over a hydrant. Use little sloping areas like the edges of driveways to get more lift.

BACKSIDE OLLIE ON VERT:
RYAN MONAHAN

OLLIE:
SHANE O'BRIEN

BACKSIDE BONELESS: SHANE O'BRIEN

BACKSIDE BONELESS: CARL ZORLAC

BOOSTS AND BONELESS

A boneless involves planting your front foot and using it to bound upwards. As you plant your front foot the back brings the tail down and the nose of the deck up in front of you. You grab the board as it comes up towards you and use your hand to keep it with your foot as you fly through the air. Release it at the peak, and bring your front foot back over the deck so you can land with both feet on the deck.

If you leap from the back foot and keep the front on the deck this is a "fast plant." You will need to kind of ollie into this one.

Bonelessnesses are nothing if you don't go into them smooth and fast. Grab first at the outside edge towards the front with your trailing hand. Experiment with other grabs. If you are small and the deck is big

FRONTSIDE BONELESS

SHANE O'BRIEN

Speed, smoothness and height are the keys to an effective boneless; note how the back foot brings the nose of the deck up to meet the hand as soon as the front foot is planted, and how the compression of the legs is released as the board is released at the top of the move, to ensure a controlled landing.

1
BULLET
2
BULLET

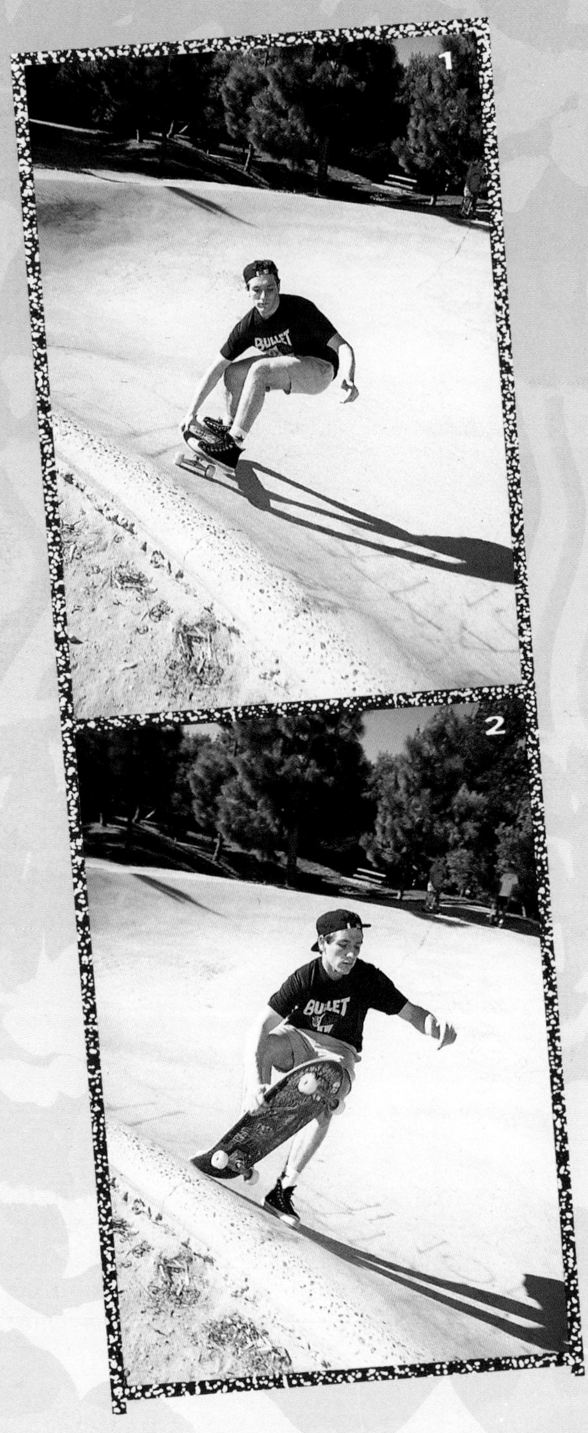

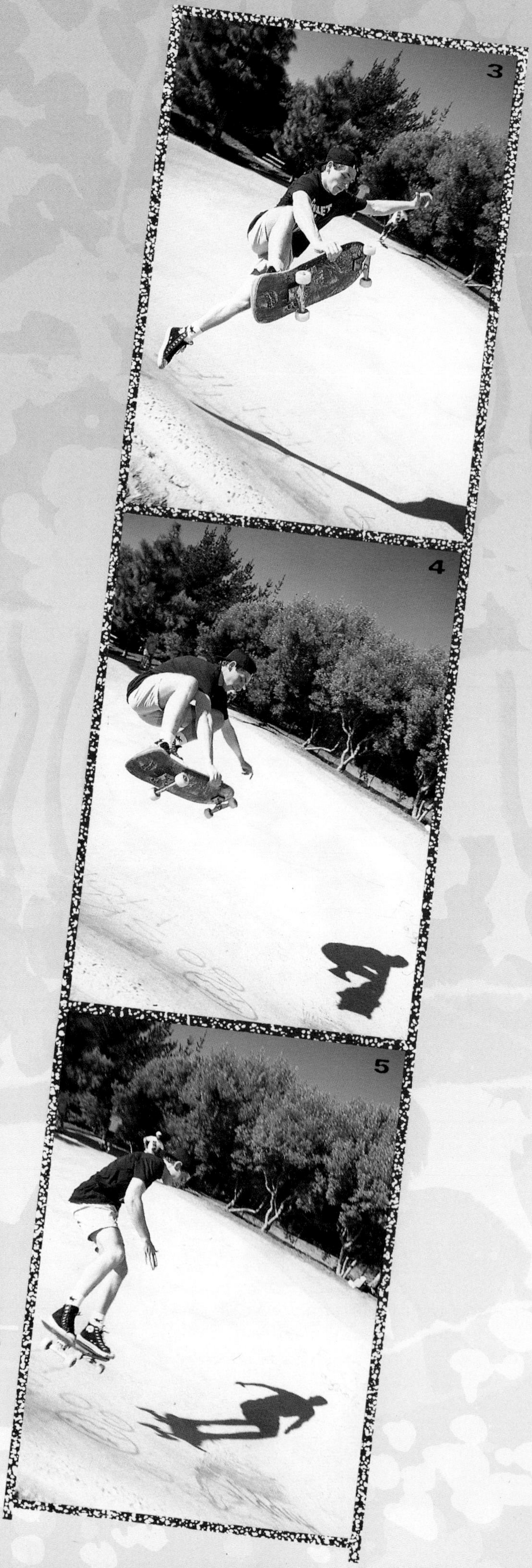
3
BULLET
4
5

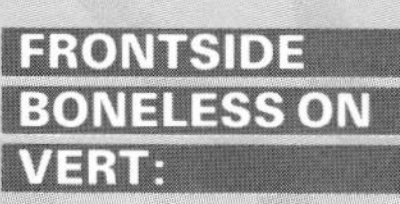

FRONTSIDE BONELESS ON VERT:
THOMAS TAILOR

180° MUTE BONELESS:
SHANE O'BRIEN
Take off forward; land fakie.

you can grab the nose with both hands.

Get the launch foot up onto things and boost off the top. Hydrants, the tops of ramps or banks, all are good for bonelessness. Try doing it with the board behind your planted foot, grabbing with the leading hand instead of the trailing one. This is a backside boneless.

Ollie as usual but plant the front foot as the nose comes up instead of using it to catch the desk. Grab the deck instead with your trailing hand (right if you are regular-footed) as it comes up, then boost up onto the board and land it. This is an ollie footplant.

There are so many permutations of bonelessness: you can grab with the other hand, or with the same hand only on the other edge of the deck, rotating it to bring the board around riding it backwards.

PUTTING IT ALL TOGETHER

Put all these moves so far described together: ollie into boosts, land it still on the bank and slide 180° out of it. Fakie one eighty ollie out of that, and then wheelie down off the bank. Invent a million variations. Look at a street or park and see how one move from one thing or area can lead into another off it, and then a third onto another, and then a fourth to lose the speed you gained off each of them.

The key to real enjoyment seems to be to learn how to draw lines and moves all over the terrain. Just doing one trick and then looking up to see who's impressed will not make you a great streetskater. Stick six together with flow and style in each street on your way to work or school, and vary it every day. That's how the legends got to be great!

BONE-UP

SHANE O'BRIEN

Approach the object at a moderate speed. Pull your board into a frontside boneless position and jump toward the object sideways; start to look at where you will pivot. While you are in the air, point the front truck down and land your front foot back on. Try to lock your arm. When you have landed it is important to get good balance to finish the move. Coming off hop off the front truck through 90° clearing your hand: the more air you get, the more you will roll out of the trick.

4
5
6
7
8
9

Through the Grinder

BOARDSLIDES AND GRINDS

Grinding the metal truck hangers was probably discovered as a technique by people who popped a wheel out off the top of a pool, and got contact between the metal and the stone coping.

This pleasant discovery came back down to the flat (a curb can be the poor man's coping). You can grind just the back truck mid kick-turn, or slide it as in a five-O grind, or grind both front and back together for a fifty-fifty grind. You can even stall on just the front for a nose pick.

The key to a good grind is a certain determination and speed, if you are coy or halfhearted you will hang up and grind your face instead. Grind anything: ollie up to get at choice spots. Good trucks can be ground right down to the steel axle before they fail. Find a kerb sloping down hill and head for it fast: feel for maximum grind and take it all the way down. Go for sparks off the steel kingpin. They make special kingpins with panhead bolts tightened by an Allen key that are great for grinds. Failing this, you can just invert your truck bolt so it is bolt to the kerb instead of nut to the kerb.

Plastic copers which fit over the trucks are generally frowned upon. You can grind away at a set of trucks for over a year generally before they die. Even then you only need to replace the kingpin and the hanger.

Boardslides are part of the same trip. Tailslides come into this too. It is quite acceptable to screw a couple of plastic rails to the underside of your deck for a smoother slide and to get a bit of extra life out of your deck. Plastic tailsavers are not so good, they can cramp your ollies and can be a bit too slidey. If you really have to make a deck last because of limited funds, then go for a thin tapering tailsaver than will not hang up. You can make a wooden one from the tail of an old trashed deck if you're clever.

If you have got the idea with truck grinds, you can easily extend this insight to cover boardslides. The positioning is different but the basic principles are the same as for truck grinds, but incorporating some of the control principles of a wheel slide.

Think of any variation of direction or orientation and you have a legitimate slide. You can even tip the board onto its edge and slide that. That's a Primo slide.

Mix slides and grinds. Find a nice painted kerb, start with a frontside grind and then slash the back wheels over for a smith grind. Small wheels make all these moves easier. Something about 97A hardness and about 60mm diameter with rounded edges is about perfect for grinds, slides, and moves involving combinations of both.

RAILSLIDE:
DONNY MYRE

RAIL SLIDE TO FAKIE

JUDE

Go into this move at any speed. Approach the curb level with it and about six inches away. Kickturn onto the curb, with the board about halfway over and stand up straight looking forward. When ready to come off, keep looking where you are going and do a 90° kickturn off the curb in the opposite direction. You should be in the same position as you were in relation to the curb at the beginning but in a fakie position.

HAND-RAIL SLIDE:
S'BANK, LONDON

SMITHGRIND:
MARK, S'BANK, LONDON

HURRICANE:
JUDE

GRABBING ON VERT:
JEFF HEDGES

360° SHOVE-SWITCH STANCE:
VINCE RODRIGUES

GRABS

You will have had plenty of occasion to grab hold of your board with one hand or other. It would take a dozen pages to illustrate all the variations, and they nearly all have names.

You can just grab your frontside rail with your trailing hand, this is about the most simple grab: it's called an indie. Still in front but with the leading hand is a slob, leading hand on the backside rail is mute, and trailing hand on the backside rail is a stalefish and is stinking hard in most circumstances. It's possible to ollie to all of these grabs and several others. Try trailing hand through the legs to the backside rail. I'm sure you can think of more. You don't need to know its name, just do it.

Whenever you do a trick grabbing one way, it is then open to try it with another grab; the permutations are manifold. Put duct tape over the thumb of your gloves to stop them wearing out on the tape: Astrodeck rubbery tape on the underside of your deck where you grab is a good idea. You can even leave those last inches at the front of the top grip-tape-free and astrodeck them. Rails help a lot too. How does that grab you?

Now you have a whole lot to put together. Grab while grinding, airing or tailsliding. Ollie into a grind or a boneless, and vary the grabs here. Do everything fast and smooth.

STALE FISH:
DAVID NEILSON

MUTE AIR:
BOD BOYLE

CRAIL TO TAIL:
MIKE YOUSSEFFOUR

LAYBACK WALL RIDE:
JOHN THOMAS

FRONTSIDE AIR:
LUCIAN HENDRICKS

GROSSMAN OLLIE:
SHANE O'BRIEN

FRONTSIDE OLLIE GRAB:
MIKE VALLEY

FRONTSIDE WALL RIDE

S'BANK LOCAL

Using your tongue as a counterbalance to maintain control is optional.

BACKSIDE WALL RIDE:

SHANE O'BRIEN

Approach the wall at an angle at a one-push speed. Start the move as soon as your front wheels are at the wall. Push your board up onto the wall by the flick of the tail and a jumping motion. With the right speed you should be riding up the wall. Come down by a compressed 180° kickturn, scraping the tail on the wall, coming out at an angle.

1

2

3

4

5

Art and Artifice

RAMP TO RAMP WALL RIDE:
JOHN THOMAS

JUMP RAMPS AND QUARTERPIPES

If you can't find the terrain you want you can always build it: whether it's just a case of putting a bit of wood over a curb or up a wall, or constructing a useful little launch ramp to take around the place, or even a full blown quarterpipe section to put up to a convenient low wall so you can get up and work the vert and the top. All these are artificial aids, but well worth it for the added fun value. It's best if nearly all these things are either disposable or indestructible.

Disposable means wear it out and cobble together another. No tears if it gets torched or stolen or a hobo moves in to live in it. This normally means making it out of scrounged timber from a new shop fitting or an old billboard. Anyone with high school woodworking skills should be able to cobble something together. Remember to try and make the bits that wear out easily, like the first front section that gets hit hard as you first mount the slope, easily replaceable. This means screwing them in place.

Indestructible means weld it out of steel. Many a small steel quarterpipe has survived years in a public park.

The transitions (curvature of the ramp) are generally small in this kind of structure: that is, of less than seven foot radius. Small transitions are tight and fast, closer to the general streetskating experience. A very small launch ramp can be kept in the garage and trucked on site on a skateboard or two.

Most wooden ramps have a structure based on two plywood formers with the curve of the slope cut into them. These are then notched to accept four-by-two (or three-by-two for a little one) cross supports which have the skating surface nailed to them. The back is supported by studwork framing, and the whole thing, apart perhaps for replaceable sections of abusable transition, is best glued and fixed with ring-annular nails (the barbed ones).

CONTEST RAMP: PHOENIX ARIZONA

STREET METHOD: SÖREN AABY

WALL RIDE TO FAKIE: JASON DICK

Ingenuity is the key to these smaller street structures. Wall riding ramps should be built to fit the wall concerned. This usually means undercutting the back to make sure the top is a good fit to the wall. It's often necessary to notch out the back to fit over a kerb at the foot of the wall. If you make it portable you can take it out and run it up against a handball wall and return it to store after the session.

GRIND TO TAIL REVERT

SHANE O'BRIEN

Go into this at moderate pace. Go into the grind and push the tail down scraping. Keep the tail down and finish the 180° turn and you should be in the drop in position. Dropping in is the same as for the smithgrind revert to complete this maneuver. Good balance is needed for good style.

BANK TO VERT:
THE LEGENDARY ERIC DRESSEN

COMPLEX RAMPS: THRASHALAND, ARIZONA

HALFPIPES AND MINI RAMPS

You may well have found by now that if a ramp or bank is facing something similar you can work back and forth and stay skating until you bail out or your legs do.

This set up, properly constituted as an integral structure, is a halfpipe. A halfpipe can be small with six foot radius transitions and about eight foot (one sheet of ply) of flat bottom between the sloping sides; in which case it is a miniramp and a lot of fun. You can take it up to vert and practice all those big ramp moves lower down, or cut it off at less than vertical and get into mellower grinds and fancy footwork.

Right at the top you can fix coping made of round scaffold tubing. Drill big holes (½") on one side so you can fix it firmly with big screws through smaller holes on the side facing the big holes. (The big holes let you get the screws in and get at them to drive them.)

A bigger ramp is much the same. A full size competition ramp might be 32 feet wide with 16 feet of flat, 10½ feet radius transitions and about 1½ feet of pure vertical on top of that. Any decent halfpipe should have at least four foot of flat platform on top of the vert for launching off, and if you really want enough room for confidence in going for difficult stuff, plus room for other skaters waiting to drop in and photographers, coaches, judges etc, you will need eight foot platforms.

A ramp in a dry climate that only has light use can be surfaced with masonite, but for a big public ramp you had better consider putting sheet steel on it for good wear. Better still, make the whole thing out of steel. Fencing the back of the platform and putting a ladder in are elementary for convenience and safety.

You don't have to stick rigidly to a simple halfpipe structure. Build them back to back and cross from one to the other. Miniramps in particular, especially indoors or in a dry climate lend themselves to exotic carpentry and convolutedly interconnecting structures.

DERBY PARK:
KEENAN-LAND, SANTA CRUZ

HALFPIPE:
WOODEN SUPERSTRUCTURE

INDY AIR:
CHRIS FARELL

MIKE:
BACKYARD RAMP, SAN JOSE

TRANSITIONAL SUPPORTS OF A HALF PIPE

SWEEPER:
BOD BOYLE (LEFT)

SMITHGRIND:
REEPS (MIDDLE LEFT)

CREEPER:
MIKE (BOTTOM LEFT)

FRONTSIDE GRIND:
JEFF HEDGES (TOP RIGHT)

SMITHGRIND:
MIKE (ABOVE)

LEIN AIR
MIKE VALLEY (RIGHT)

RAD

Vert

BACKSIDE AIR:
TONY ALVA

NATURAL VERT

The essential and original natural vert has to be a pool. Not a nasty new square olympic tank: a mellow, organically curved beauty. She gets drained once or twice a year, up in the hills in an empty villa, or low season on the coast in a hotel. Sometimes you come across the perfect pool alone in the grounds of a long demolished villa, isolated, quiet and perfect for carving and grinding.

They come in a hundred shapes: kidneys, right- and left-handed; rounded squares like a big TV screen; keyholes like the now 'dozed Ghost Bowl in our pics; frighteningly tight squares with convex corners.

Pools are about carving and grinding. When the day gets on you, go for the inaccessible spots: the shallow end walls; grind the hips, over the steps frontside; big old frontside airs dropped onto the coping for a frightening grind.

The original style is to work the coping and tiles with your body low and horizontal. The feeling is of weightlessness, time on the tiles and coping is stretched. The newer styles involve getting your centre of gravity high out over the edge above the coping, working it like a ramp. Some pools have a mile of vert and see off the attempts to dominate them like a halfpipe. Just to get a fat grind is to win for the day.

Riding pools is about speed and confidence: that first fast drop into the deep end and the whiplash speed up onto the vert either chills the blood or stokes it to confidence. Things happen faster than you can believe, then suddenly time stops and you are up on the tiles or two wheels out in a fifty-fifty on the coping.

Hunting for pools is a sport in itself. Some zealots even take to the air over likely areas. The law may not be on your side: be careful.

Fullpipes and drainage pans and ditches are country terrain. Big fast laid-back reservoirs for surfstyle fast carves and slides, or massive great fullpipes in the sides of dams or standing alone in the desert waiting to be buried forever in the ground. Fullpipes have been ridden when parked on a transporter. A skating friend of the author's who worked on a vast hydroelectric scheme in Europe would skate the 25 foot pipes from the top to the bottom for miles down the steep incline, knowing that they would very soon be lost to the fishes.

Natural vert is often transient. It can be right in the city where a thoughtful architect has specified a concrete bank running up to a vertical wall in some futuristic development. Ride it while you can. Quit before anyone minds about you, and come again on a different shift.

TONY ALVA: *In at the deep end at the Ghost Bowl, working the sides and coping with the body low and horizontal, dominating the pool with carves and grinds.*

VERT MOVES

The easiest vert moves to start with are the verticalized developments of miniramp and street moves. Grinds, slides, bonelesses and other boosts, all work fine on the vert. One of the main new lessons is that moves that demanded that you pull or pop them hard off the skating surface can be floated smoothly up and out of the ramp. Concentrate on the speed and let it work for you. Coping can just serve to pop you away from the surface and speed does the rest.

The basic workhorse is the simple fakie up and down like a child's swing, working up height before a kickturn or two. As you get better you can put the tail on the coping and, stepping on smartly, drop in from the top. There is no halfway. At the first step you are vertical on the platform, in the next instant you must be fully committed and horizontal to the floor, getting on down that transition. To be meek with this move is to slam badly. If you bail, try and slide out on your knees. Thickly padded, hard-shelled pads are a must for this.

When you have made something one way try it the other. Frontside after backside. Try it to fakie or from fakie. There is always too much temptation when skating with a lot of others to drop straight in and go for the big one: mellow out, work up speed and string a few basics together and then try for the big one. Then you've loosened up and if you slam it's not so bad.

Ramp embellishments like tombstones, channels and the like can be brought into play to develop variations on well-worked themes. String them together.

VERT SKATER:
PALACE BOY (TOP)

LIPSLIDE:
BOD BOYLE (MIDDLE)

FRONTSIDE ROCK:
BOB BLAIR (LEFT)

BACKSIDE DISASTER

CHRIS FARELL

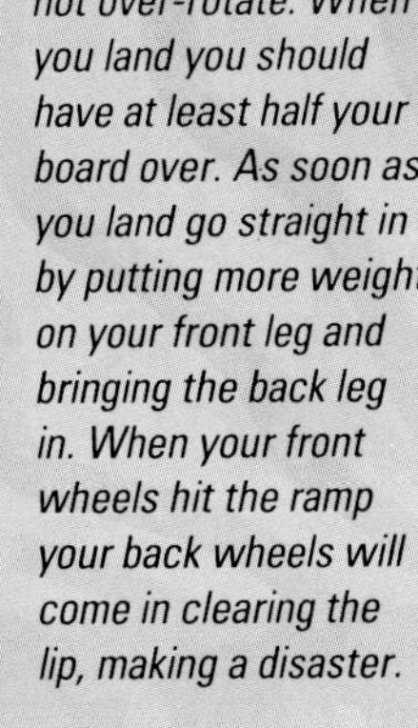

Approach the wall at a moderate speed. Throw your body onto the lip through 180°. Do not over-rotate. When you land you should have at least half your board over. As soon as you land go straight in by putting more weight on your front leg and bringing the back leg in. When your front wheels hit the ramp your back wheels will come in clearing the lip, making a disaster.

ROCK FAKIE

CHRIS FARELL

This move is similar to Fakie move but harder. When you put the board over the lip push down slightly with the front leg, to get the back wheels off. When you have, stop, push the back leg down and take the weight off the front leg. The back wheels should hit the ramp and you will roll back into the ramp clearing the lip with the front truck. Weight distribution is important. Stay straight on this move all the way: don't twist, and stand up for good balance.

1

DROP IN

ANDY VOST

Proceed to put the board over the lip. Stand on the board normally. Drop into the ramp at a moderate pace by pushing your weight on your leading leg all the way until your front wheels meet the ramp. Do not push too quickly or too slowly: it has to be moderately for good speed.

4

5

2

3

BLUNT

BOD BOYLE

Roll up to the lip slowly in a straight line. Let your back wheels roll onto the platform and put pressure on the tail to balance and stop the board. Grab the board in a backside air position, then hop back into the ramp by pulling and pushing with your leg and arm. When coming in, do not get too much air and land in a straight line, standing up straight.

SMITHGRIND REVERT

JIM NAMBA

Approach the wall as you would a grind. Go into a grind and push the rail down early with your toes. Hold it there by locking your legs and standing over the back truck. When you are ready to come in, let your board roll into the ramp normally. As your front wheels hit the ramp, start to rotate board and body through 180°, by pushing the board round with the back leg doing more work. As you go through the move keep your shoulders square with the nose and board. Do not over-rotate. Excellent balance is needed for this one.

INVERT:
BRIAN PENNINGTON

STRAIGHT-LEGGED INVERT:
LOUIE

VERT MOVES #2: PLANTS

The first principle of a handplant is that you are not using your arm to get you up there. Your vertical speed gets you up and your hand gets you planted down to control and develop the work. Airs come before plants.

All the familiar variations apply to handplants. All the different grabs and directions can be attempted. In one way, plant, and out the other. This is where your imagination can have full play. The basic plant – grabbed with the leading hand at the frontside and planting the rear – becomes an eggplant when the leading hand is planted instead. If you can do all the permutations that can come to your mind, your mind is either very limited or you are one of the top few skaters in the world.

INVERT

JEFF HEDGES

Approach the lip with speed and at a slight angle. Grab your board firmly with your leading arm and at the same time grab the lip close to your board with the other arm. Your board will go out. At the same time push up with your arm on the coping. Aim to go directly above the coping for good balance. When ready to come in, use the extended arm to pull you round to the other side from which you started. Pull yourself into the lip; if necessary, pull yourself over the lip. Land all wheels together on the ramp, then let go of the board and coping and stand up.

EGGPLANT

BOD BOYLE

Go up the wall as if you were doing an alley ooped indy air. Aim for the coping with your planting hand, plant your hand and push your body up as for an invert. Coming in is the same technique as for an invert, except that you land it on the right-hand side of your planting hand for regulars. Pull it in as much as you can.

SAD PLANT

JEFF HEDGES

This move is similar to the invert. As you go into the plant, straighten your leading leg until it locks and tuck your back leg in. The more you straighten and lock your legs, the better it will be. Grab the rail near the back truck. When ready to come in, return both legs to normal position: don't take it slow. Land this in the same way as the invert.

ELGUARIAL

BOD BOYLE

Go up the wall backward and crouch down. As you come to the lip grab your board with your hand. As you start turning, plant your other hand on the lip. Then spin your body round with your shoulders and bring the board round holding it tight. All your weight should be put onto planting hand. As you come to land the move, push away from the lip with the planting hand, to land coming in like an invert.

SAD PLANT:
LANCE MOUNTAIN

ONE FOOT SADPLANT:
JEFF HEDGES

ONE-FOOTED ANDRECT:
JEFF HEDGES

FRIGID AIR:
ADRIAN DEMAIN

EXTREME VERT

A simple indy air floated high frontside across the ramp begs a million variations. Grab it stalefish after ollieing into it; land it in a fakie. Take it right around 540° in the now old and celebrated Mctwist; still only accomplished by a few dozen souls.

As airs get higher there is more time for extreme contortions like the Japan air or for theatricals like Christ airwalks with both feet right off the board which is held out at arm's length while the skater soars for the sky. Having the confidence to know you have the time to fully style these moves, before getting everything back where it should be for a smooth re-entry, marks out the able from the aspiring with this kind of action. Then these moves too are varied; ridden backwards, feet switched, tricks combined in the air or landed on the coping with a smash and a grind. There are no limits. Boards tossed around during handplants for Dutch plants (like a windmill). Both hands on the coping and the board poised on the feet for a quick walk across the platform and back in, and you have a ho-ho plant.

Practice on the ramp has to be supplemented with hours spent juggling the board in the hands or onto your back for a foot juggling session. The balance of the deck has to be as well-known to you as your own face. There are no shortcuts.

The consistent competition winner has a balanced routine of airs, liptricks, plants and even perhaps slides on the flat bottom. His or her runs have to be matched to the occasion. The right amount to impress the judges and make the cut, with something in reserve for the finals and maybe for the skate-off for the top place. Champions impress in all areas. Many use their mastery of freestyle and street moves to expand their ramp routines.

Besides all this it has to be more satisfying to work the whole envelope; to be able to combine all aspects of the art in one halfpipe run. After all, the essence of this business is that the skate and the ramp are as simple as can be imagined. The variation and development come from the skate artist.

AIR WALK:
BOD BOYLE

INDY AIR:
BOD BOYLE

METHOD AIR:
BOD BOYLE

FAKIE OLLIE STALE FISH

CHRIS FARELL

Approach the lip at any speed. Pop the wheels off the coping and stay compressed. As the board is going up, grab your rails solid and pull them toward you with your leading arm. On landing hold the board tight and release the board halfway past the lip. It is optional to angle your leading leg inward, to make it easier to get a firm grab.

METHOD AIR:
LOCAL BOY AT LOU'S, SANTA CRUZ

MCTWIST (540):
DAVID NELSON

MCTWIST (540):
TONY MAGNUSSON

GAY TWIST

Go up the wall with speed. On the way up the wall, twist your body and get ready to spin. As you approach the lip, spin your shoulders quicker than your body. Then pop the back wheels off the coping and continue the spinning. As soon as you pop out, grab the board in the middle of the rail and hold it tight, and let the board catch up with your shoulders. Once you have completed the 360° motion, take it in as best you can, landing it like an air. Remember the trick is in the shoulders.

VARIAL HANDPLANT:
JEFF HEDGES

STALE FISH:
CHRIS FARELL

MADONNA:
CARL ZORLAC

Freestyle

ONE-FOOTED 50 50: WALLACE SUEYOSHI

ON THE FLAT

As the other extreme from vert there is freestyle or flatland skating. The first skaters could not go very fast so they messed around with complex footwork. One man, Rodney Mullen, took this into a different dimension in the early eighties and he still keeps all the other freestylers worldwide in his wake.

A freestyle setup is much smaller than a street deck with narrower trucks and little hard wheels. Most do not even have concave; just a simple kicktail and a long overhang on the nose.

There are only a couple of rules in freestyle. The first is that you have to use a skateboard with four wheels, two trucks, and a deck. The other is that you should confine yourself to the flat.

Because of this simplicity the variations are almost limitless. There are tricks just involving variations of tic-tacs. Tricks have evolved around flicking the board over sideways with your feet: kickflips. Ollies figure large, but can be combined with other flips or spun and varied in other ways. If you turn the board up and stand on the trucks, no-one will frown. So go on, stand on your hand and throw the whole thing in the air. Ride handstand, do a flip with your hands. Stand on the wheels with the board on its side and slide it along like this.

Tricks may be stationary, they may be done while rolling at running pace. Anything goes and variation is the key. Freestylers often practice for hours in the kitchen, the garage, in the parking lot or down at the beach. The best are often semi-solitary obsessives.

Competitions consist of runs lasting a few minutes, ideally judged by other freestylers who can appreciate the more esoteric and rapid tricks that only reveal themselves to the practiced eye of a fellow skater or the slomo replay.

A freestyle deck is worth having even if you never plan to be an expert. Tricks can be learned on any flat space, even in the office. The whole setup is small enough to go in a bag, and a lot of street and ramp tricks first saw the light of day on a skinny little freestyle deck in a sheltered parking lot.

Shin pads are the special freestyler's extra: the spinning board often breaks away from its planned trajectory mid-flip and homes in on an unprotected shin. Good ankle padding is worth looking for in any skateshoe, but with freestyle it can keep you skating instead of having to lay off flips for a week or so while a great fat bruise heels.

VARIAL SPINNER: WALLACE SUEYOSHI (TOP)

540° SHOVIT: DON BROWN (BOTTOM)

360° BACKSIDE 50 50

ANTHONY SEDILLO

Start this move stationary and with feet transposed, leading foot on the tail and trailing foot on the underside of the board. As you pull the board round with your feet through 90° the feet should change to the normal stance. The foot on the underside of the board should slide down to stand on the back truck and the foot on the tail slides up the grip tape onto the nose bolts to be leading the move. The board should now be vertical. You should be springing all the time to reach the 360°; lower the board slightly in the opposite direction to get more force to complete the move. When the board has gone through 360°, push the board over and then down with the nose and jump back on the normal riding side in the normal position.

HANDSTAND KICKFLIP

ANTHONY SEDILLO

This move requires speed. Push yourself into the handstand, with hands in the same grabbing position on the nose and tail, fingers wrapped around the edges of each end. When you are in the handstand and ready to come down, get ready to take your weight off your hands and bring your knees toward the body. Then flip the board 360° toward your feet with your fingers at the same time bringing your feet down and in to meet it. As you are weightless and upside down, you need to bring your knees in fast and aim to land standing up right. This is a truly gymnastic move.

WALKING THE DOG

WALLACE SUEYOSHI

Position your back foot on the tail or nose, front foot in the middle of the board. Keep the front foot in the middle of the board and use it as a pivot point. Rotate your body counter-clockwise, and put your foot on the opposite end. Now do a 180° kickturn in the clockwise direction. Repeat as many times as required. Try to get this move smooth and fast, then you can build on variations.

CASPERS

WALLACE SUEYOSHI

Position your front foot parallel to your left side (regular footed) and perpendicular to your other foot on the nose or tail. Now press down and scoop the board on to your front foot. Now that the board is upside down, put your back foot in the area behind your truck. Let it bounce off the ground and catch it. Land it back onto the wheels by spinning it on the long or short axis of the board.

1 2 3 4 5 6 7 8 9

180° SPINNER

WALLACE SUEYOSHI

Set up on the rail – have the nose by your back foot. Position your feet at a 45° angle. Keep your front foot over the wheel; your back foot by the end of the board past your wheel. Put the toes on the side. Now compress, jump up and kick the back foot sideways. The board should be spinning. Now land it.

1

2

3

4

POGOS

WALLACE SUEYOSHI

The easiest way is to do a wheelie stall, front foot in front of the back foot, which should be by the truck holes. Now with your back hand, throw the board straight over, transfer the board to your front hand, and land on the truck with your back foot. Hang on, and bounce around for a while. Come down as for a finger-flip.

STREET-FREESTYLE FUSION

There are so many ways that freestyle moves can filter out into streetstyle. Many of today's top streetstylers owe a lot to freestyle. Flips first tried on the little deck can be simplified and applied to the top of a wall with a street deck. Plants first attempted on the ground may be applied to the kerb or mixed with moves on a miniramp.

An infusion of freestyle rule-breaking can lend spice to the descent of a long smooth shallow hill with few variations. String a whole load of rolling freestyle tricks together or cut back up the slipe and pull a plant on the stall. Go for a funny finger flip during a big air off the launch ramp. You could try and carve that bank on your hands.

Little wheels are the thing for tight, freestyle-inspired streetstyle. They also lend themselves to grinds etc. so a set of well rounded freestyle wheels is often the business for your street deck, whatever your style. Rollerskate wheels are not to be despised in this field either.

FORTY THREE: *Ollie, kickflip and no-comply variations inhabit the street-freestyle fusion zone.*

SLALOM AND HILL RIDING

Pretty early on folk discovered that just blasting down a great hill is one of the major rushes. Early pioneers like Bill Bahne were skiers as well as surfers and so the idea of downhill racing and slalom came naturally to them.

Tight slalom on the flat or on a shallow slope is practiced on a slim, flexible, fiber-glass-reinforced deck with no nose or tail to foul the free movement of the wheels. People jack up the angle of their narrow trucks to get even more steer. The speed of some racers will give you a nosebleed just watching.

In practice, if you have a reasonable setup and don't worry too much about knocking over a few cones, it's easy enough to get quite quick through the cones or cans that you lay out about six feet apart, down a gentle slope at first. Let your body follow the straight line down over the cones as closely as possible while your feet and hips pump the little board through the gates. As with everything else, once you get the knack it's just a case of training and a refinement and tuning of things like your foot position and stance.

There are two main stances used in slalom. The commonest has the feet almost together and parallel to each other, slightly angled across the deck so the side-to-side steering is a matter of the toe of one foot acting against the heel of the other across the deck. A variation of this involves having the feet completely parallel to the direction of travel like a skier, giving the option of working the weight from foot to foot alternately to give a very natural "walking" pump action.

The other stance has the front foot over the front truck, as for a street deck and the other foot – or even just the ball of the other foot – over the other truck, powering it from side to side in a thrusting, pump style that relies on power to get you fast through the course rather than the flow of the ski style.

Both styles have their fans and some switch styles depending on the course. The second "surf style" is the one for the tight flat runs, and the ski style wins on more open downhill courses.

SLALOM BOARD

Whichever way, all movement has to depend on the whole body, especially hips and knees, rather than just the ankles. Arms are good as counterbalances and it's always worth noting how you use them, so as to be sure you are not wasting effort just waving them about rather than making them assist the general flow.

Giant slalom is more akin to ski slalom. You need a big wide hill and cones or gates spread down the slope to test the ability to control speed as well as just to power on.

DOWNHILL STYLING: MIKE JOHN

Wheels are softer than for tight slalom, and slide control is as important as pumping power. A fast run demands a lot of courage as the one who resists the temptation to slow too much and takes the cleanest line is often the fastest.

DOWNHILL RACING

The simplest form of downhill racing can be fairly dangerous and requires good pads or leathers. A whole pack of skaters just heads off down a closed-off road or a section of motor racing track and see who gets down first. Slipstreaming and careful selection of line wins the race after the initial shunting has sorted out the frontrunners from the pack. Although it seems dangerous, properly managed it can be safe enough and exciting to watch as well as to take part in.

Lugers race individually on special long skates that you lie on in a prone position. Speeds in excess of 70mph are quite common. Racers also stage timed runs, standing up like downhill ski racing.

A hill is a great source of thrills on a regular board once you have learned to slide off extra speed. Great sweeping carves and drifted slides punctuated with high speed ollies and stages skated fakie make for maximum thrill. The only problem is finding safe and legal auto-free terrain. Many motor racing circuits, especially in Europe, have steep gradients and will let a group of you hire a section for the weekend for a reasonable charge. Often the steep section is not used for certain types of motor racing. Sometimes they have special hillclimb sections that can be skated in reverse.

Legal Rushes

STREET SKATERS: *The perplexing truth dawns that some people use sidewalks for walking.*

SKATE AS TRANSPORT

It's important to remember that a skate is not just for top-level competitive sport. It is a simple and effective mode of local transport, and an air traveller with a skate can often be the last off the plane and the first home, because where it's tolerated these types of places are perfect for skate transport.

The joy of a skate over a bike or rollerskates is that you can flip it up into your hand and become a pedestrian, or a bus or train passenger in a blink of an eye. Skating to school or work is valuable exercise and you can switch from the simple, straight scoot when you're in a hurry, to a complex sidewalk dance when the sun is shining and time is plentiful.

To be a real skateboarder you don't have to learn to McTwist. You just have to be good enough to have fun, and if you take it easy this should come from day one.

The whole thing about skating is that if the local authorities take a liberal attitude, the urban scene can become a playground for a skater. The only tough truth is to remember that cars or large numbers of pedestrians – especially very old or very young ped's – do not mix with skateboards.

SAFETY AND SURVIVAL

In some cities and states ordinances have been passed banning or severely limiting skateboarding; sometimes this is a result of fear born from misunderstanding or perhaps even the result of an accident involving an imprudent skater.

Making your skating low impact can help ease and prevent this. If a place is skateable but it might not be allowed, don't stay too long or session in large numbers or be noisy. This way you will not be a problem to anyone in authority often enough to necessitate someone "doing something about it."

The same goes for private backyard ramps: neighbours can be upset if you are generally uncool about it. If you have trouble with a pathologically intolerant neighbour you may have to consult a laywer; it's probably not worth the effort, but that's up to you.

In matters of personal safety common sense and self-preservation should be enough. Just gloves and simple pads will do for basic street skating. On a high ramp you are not only at risk from falling, but you have to watch out for flying boards. A high velocity deck can kill. Wear a helmet and you will skate better, even if your bravado says you don't mind, your subsconscious will know the risk and make you jell out, whereas wearing a good, comfortable, light helmet and pads would give you the class to stay on to the end.

With extreme downhill racing, leathers and a proper helmet are essential if you don't want your skin peeling off in a high-speed slide. It is all just plain common sense.

Always check your gear before you skate. Tighten wheel nuts, check truck fixing bolts and check the trucks themselves for cracks. Make sure your laces are tied, stupid things like that often make for the gnarliest accidents.

And if a policeman or similar grabs you because he thinks you shouldn't be doing it there, be polite and reasonable: he may be right, and your demeanor may get you let off. You may be right but your bad demeanor may blacken his attitude to skaters in general and lead to a bad time later for someone else. Because skating takes place in the same bits of the world as real life, it often rubs up against it. Common sense can ensure plenty of good times and happy hours skating with your bros. Have fun and may your wheels not jam on too many nasty little rocks.

Index

The figures in italics refer to captions.